Tabby In Elysium: A Mock Poem

Friedrich Wilhelm Zachariae

In the interest of creating a more extensive selection of rare historical book reprints, we have chosen to reproduce this title even though it may possibly have occasional imperfections such as missing and blurred pages, missing text, poor pictures, markings, dark backgrounds and other reproduction issues beyond our control. Because this work is culturally important, we have made it available as a part of our commitment to protecting, preserving and promoting the world's literature. Thank you for your understanding.

TABBY

IN

ELYSIUM,

A MOCK POEM,

FROM THE GERMAN OF

F. W. ZACHARIAE,

BY

R. E. RASPE.

LONDON:

PRINTED FOR THE TRANSLATOR,
BY H. GOLDNEY;
AND SOLD BY T. CADELL IN THE STRAND.
M.DCC.LXXXI.

[Price One Shilling and Sixpence.]

ADVERTISEMENT.

THE German Muse has since these last forty years generously emulated the muses of Greece, of Rome, and of Britannia. True to nature, the first teacher and object of all, and strong by her national idiom, which is polished, expressive, and musical, she has inspired many of her favourites, and produced successful attempts, which have stood the trial of candid criticism, and will bear even the harder proof of translation. The late professor Zachariae at Brunswick shared her favours; and it is presumed that a translation of his Tabby may afford some amusement to those ladies and gentlemen, whose taste and applause are not confined to climates and countries, and whose judgment is not prejudiced against any poetical performance but that of scandal and of indecency. To them it is humbly inscribed, together with some other works of the same poet, which will appear in this very form unless the Translator should be told: Proceed no further!

ERRATA.

Page 1. Line 3. for Cocvytus *read* Cocytus
    4.   3.   ſhakehaired *read* ſnakehaired
   24.   25.   reſound *read* reſound of

TABBY
IN
ELYSIUM.

SING, smiling Muse! the heroic atchievements and the lamentable fate of an immortal Tabby; he passed the black banks of Cocytus; as other heroes his bones were entombed in marble.

And thou, gentle Rosaura! for three hours thy tears bewailed the untimely end of thy favourite—longer than many buxom widows bewail the loss of their gouty husbands! Animate my song with thy conquering eye, which enflames the heart;

heart; smile boldness into the Muse's breast, when she hears the Stygian floods roaring under her steps, and ventures to mix with the melancholy crowds of skipping shades that wait the pleasure of Charon.

Amidst the mossy towers of an old castle on the gay banks of Albia lived old Baron Raban, and with him Rosaura his niece. There was not in that neighbourhood a lady more beautiful than his Rosaura. The Graces were not more charming, nor Venus more lovely when first she stept forth from the waves. She was the uncle's darling; what she desired, he would command. Yet her desires were but few, and that the more engaged the affection of the domestic and parsimonious man. Pleased with herself in peaceful retirement, she spent her days not troubled by envy or darkened by pride. Two social companions shared her apartments, a sleek striped tabby and a talkative gawdy coloured poll, that came over the ocean, and chatted away many hours of his mistress's with an eloquence and improvement as effectual as that of empty macaronies.

Parting winter had just then shook from his stormy wings his last showers of hail. Spring rode triumphant over the gently waving variegated carpets of violets and tulips; and Philomela tried interrupted preludes to loftier strains, under the half-green shrubs, when crimson Aurora arose in the
eastern

eastern sky; piercing breezes preceded her; with shrill howlings they roared around the lonely castle, and bid the sulky housemaid to fetch fuel and to light fires again. Tabby the rake came home now over the roofs. All the night long he had roamed through lonely barns and dispersed legions of rats. Their blood had drenched his sharp armed jaws and drunk with victory, he had sported and rolled on the heaps of the slain. Slily he stole into the room, when the chambermaid came with the boiling kettle, to wake her dear mistress to tea. She found her still slumbring; she dropt again the rustling curtain, and left the lady's apartment on the tip of her toe; tired from his nocturnal adventures Tabby laid himself down at the fire-side, stretched his lion-paws, and soon after fell unconcerned asleep. His fancies roamed in golden dreams. He saw the forms of pretty pussies assembled about him; and heard the sighs of tenderness and affection which on his account resounded at night from mossy roofs and ivy-clad tottering walls; then he thought himself lying familiarly in the lap of Rosaura, by her lovely hand coaxed and stroaked; and envied by some noble blockhead, or some spruce Ensign. Vain fancies! He was doomed no longer to visit the caverns of rats, or the haunts of his pussies! No more to be rocked in Rosaura's arms, nor purring to fall asleep! One of those furies, that with burning torch enflame the hearts of Xantippe's to quarrel with their husbands: Alecto steered her way

back.

back to Tartarus. Horrid and black she rode on a fetid cloud, and passed by Rosaura's windows. Prattling Polly was in his wire cage safe; he cried, "Ugly Monster," when the shake-haired fury passed by. Furies too have in their horrid bosoms the pride of beauty, and Alecto was lady enough to be highly provoked at that foul reproach. She mutter'd: "Thy inso-
"lence, villain, I might easily punish. My resentment might
"wring thy treacherous throat! This hell-lighted torch might
"burn thee to ashes! But thou art too insignificant for a god-
"dess immortal! Begone, then, and abuse me at leisure in
"the stomach of Tabby that sleeps there. To him I doom
"thee a victim."

Raving she approached our sleeping Tabby, inspired him with her bloody revenge and spoke to him smoothly: "Is't possible?
"Thou snorest here at the fire-side? Thou pride of all tab-
"bies, canst thou thus forget, that honour calls thee to glo-
"rious actions, and to victory which no other Tabby yet
"attempted? So nearly and nobly related to tigers, wilt thou
"pursue only the cowardly host of mice, and with powerful
"fangs destroy only long-tailed rats? Dost thou not thirst for
"nobler blood? Behold yon favourite of Rosaura, how saucy
"he bids thee defiance in his golden cage; whenever he pleases
"he calls thee names, nay often he dares to utter foul lan-
"guage and curses against thy Rosaura. Too indulging she hears
"him

" him and rewards him with smiles, with fondness and flat-
" tery, whilst thou art forgot and neglected. Do not suffer the
" chattering coxcomb any longer to engross thy lady's favour
" or to mimick thy manly voice in order to ridicule thee!
" The cage is but a feeble and idle defence of the parasite!
" Many canary birds were torn in their cages by thy gallant
" ancestors! Make haste then; destroy the talkative slanderer
" and his plumage so gay, which makes him proud, give it
" to the winds, that they may blow it about, and proclaim
" thy revenge and thy triumph."

Thus the Fury. Tabby abruptly awaked; looked round with fiery eyes, and roared for blood. As from the top of Olympus a flash of lightning rushes down to the plains and shatters the blowing tree, under whose shades the shepherd's harmonious horn had often delighted the ear; so Tabby started from the fireside to destroy his odious rival, and swift as a panther he leapt on the top of the cage. The tenant was terrified, and dropt to the bottom, and cried " Murther, assistance, " and mercy!" Yet must he have fallen a prey to Tabby's attack, had not old Raban overheard the wild noise of the scuffle, and hastened to the place, where assistance was wanted. The trembling hand of the Lord happened to be armed with his knotty walking stick; and when he beheld Tabby, crampt with his fangs over the cage with murtherous intent, he laid it with manly force on the skull of Rosaura's favourite. The cruel Parcæ cut at once his ninefold life: Tabby dropt dead to the ground, on him the cage, over it the Baron; and the apartment was shaken by the thundring ruin.

Wild was the noise. It frightened and awakened Rosaura; in her night gown she flew to her apartment, where astonished she beheld this scene of bloody confusion. Thrice rung with frightful sound the silver bell through the echoing castle; and before Betty arrived, Rosaura had already helped the old hero to her velvet arm chair.——When he had breathed and recovered his voice, he directed it thundering to the lady in tears. " Behold the dog there," he said; " He was about " murthering our Polly! but heavens! I am a man still! " there he lies dead----the ravenous villain! I warrant he " won't dare it again!" Thus bragging in his pride, he shook thrice his victorious club over the body of Tabby. But the lady cried aloud; she hid her fair face and her tears in an handkerchief, and sunk in an arm chair. Muse, record the tender lamentations of the mourning lady, nor do thou forget the vociferous cries of Betty; for she came and echoed her lady.

" Poor

"Poor Tabby!" sighed Rosaura, "miserable indeed is the "fate which deprives me of thee!—Inglorious in the bloom of "thy life—Slain with a stick, ignobly and cruel—Slain by the "same hands which gave thee to me! Is there no life remain- "ing? And are thy green sparkling eyes shut for ever? Shall "I no longer stroak thy manly whiskers, nor rub sparks from "thy silken coat in the dark. Thy bent back, and anticks and "capers will no more delight me!" Thus Rosaura; and the chambermaid went on, "O Glory of Tabbies! lordly were thy "looks! they expressed thy rank above the mean bred Tab- "bies of farmers! Thy red spangled collar was the envy of "all the cats around. It became thee! Now thou art doomed "to rot, and thy collar with thee. Too pretty for rottenness "and decay; I shall take it to myself! nor shall it go to be "lost! Ah, thy purple blood trickles from thy head! Indeed "thou art dead——for ever, poor Tabby, thou art dead!"

At this lamentation the grief of the lady broke out afresh. Even the old man joined in tears. He took the hand of his niece and led her away from this scene of sorrow; and Betty cried louder, "Poor Tabby!" The lady replied sobbing, "Poor "Tabby!" "Tabby!" echoed the walls; "Tabby! Tabby!" the parrot, who forgave his enemy.

Alecto

Alecto beheld it with infernal delight; hissing, she rushed through the darkening day, and plunged in the flood of Orcus.

CANTO II.

As soon as the coast was clear, and Betty was left mistress of the room, the mask of mourning dropt; nor was she any longer the echo of Rosaura's grief. Well pleased she looked down on Tabby's body, for she had hated him full heartily when alive. Thus self contented the cruel conqueror views the field of battle, and feeds his eyes on blood; high riding on his prancing neighing horse he leaps elated over the heaps of bodies slain, and when the trumpet of his conquering troops sounds all around, he deems himself to be a God. Scoffing, the malicious chambermaid pushed the bloody carcase with her feet; and with hands profane she tore from its neck the purple collar, embroidered with silver flowers and foliage, looked at it with avarice mean, rolled it up and said, " Thank heavens! thou
" villainous creature! thou hast-broken thy treacherous neck!
" Happy,

"Happy, thrice happy! that I behold thee thus humbled! I am
"sure, that henceforth my lady cannot rock thee in her lap, nor
"kifs thee with fondnefs. Fie! Shame! How could her beauti-
"ful lips prefs kiffes upon thee! How could her delicate hands be
"pleafed to ftroak thee! Be gone now, thou ravenous thief! Steal
"partridges and dainties, which I faved for thy betters! Be gone,
"now, thou glutton! Kill pigeons and parrots!

Thus fhe infulted poor Tabby. Too fuddenly changes the fmooth language of courtiers, who have nothing to fear or to hope. Betty opened the window, took Tabby by a hind leg, and threw him on the dunghill. Thus formerly the ftatues of Tyrants tumbled from their pedeftals; and the terrors of Rome, maimed marbles, were thrown into noifome canals.

Meanwhile Rofaura was gone from the afflicting fcene, and ftayed with her good natured old uncle. He attempted with kindnefs to leffen her forrow. He fpoke of a jaunt to the Wells, promifed new fafhioned ftuffs, and played on her fancy with Soucies and Lilacs. Comforted and gay fhe returned to her apartment; unmindful of her favourite, fhe did not think of his burial; and fate down to her toilet. Boxes opened, and drawers; the irons heated in coals, and clouds of powder were puffed around her. Soon after rattling coaches rolled in the court, and glittering ftrangers arrived. The folemn fmell of coulis and paftry, and noble

D   viands,

viands spread from the kitchen; and the gay company enjoyed the long dinner, well seasoned with easy jokes. The sparkling glasses went round amongst the squires, till they reeled and bright Hesperus twinkled in the West; whilst Rosaura at the harpsichord, surrounded by listning admirers, charmed the flying hours with song and with music. 'Twas thus that grief and mourning were subdued and forgotten.

The groping soul of poor Tabby had hastened to hell. Forgive and vouchsafe, ye Stygian powers, ye lonely shades! Thou, Chaos and Plegethon, and ye vast caves of the dead, that I dare to disclose to the eye of the living the unfathomable depths of the abyss. Tabby marched on through thick Cimmerian darkness, over the wide and gloomy plains of the Plutonian domains. He reached the purlieus of Hell. There dwell bitter complaints, revenging sorrow, heart-felt pains, pale mortal diseases, old age in sadness, hunger, poverty, fear, and despair. Frightful visions lorded it here, war and snake hairy discord. Dreadful dreams fluttered in the gloom of rustling elms. Terrible monsters roamed, crowded herds of Centaurs ferocious, of Gorgons, of Hyænas, and of disgustful harpies. Tabby hastened, frightened and trembling through all these horrors, to the Stygian shore; in sadness and forlorn he skipped along the banks of dark Cocytus. The flood roared irresistible and wild towards the gates of death. Here plied dark Charon, the squallid old ferryman; his grey beard uncombed and wild,

reaches

reaches down to his girdle. Sulky he sate in his barge, and steered it slowly against the current of roaring floods, to the shore, where thousands of souls had crowded to meet him. Here walked in promiscuous throng, princes, players, and poets, whores and nuns, goldmakers, robbers, attorneys and doctors, with sextons and well-pleased heirs. There were souls of ladies of fashion, with a retinue of lapdogs, of cats and of parrots, whilst the shades of neglected children were left on the shore, and implored their mothers in vain. With that proud contempt, which is deemed to become the lady of fashion, the mothers turned them off, for their favourites in life, their sweet pretty lapdogs. As when winter comes on, and Boreas wars through the forest, and sweeps the skipping leaves, decayed and dry, in thick clouds through the valley; or as vociferous swarms of wandering sea fowls assemble and cover the waves on the coast of Thule: thus the shades hurried to the river, and lifted their begging hands up to Charon, who took some in his barge, and drove others back with his oar; for the surly fellow does not ferry any souls over the Stygian waters and the floods of Cocytus but those who have had the last honour of burial on earth. Poor Tabby's shade was likewise rejected. With grief and with sorrow he remained on the banks, and hoped for a passage in vain. He ventured into the water and tried to cross it by swimming; but Charon did catch him with his oar, and drove him back to the land. Desponding and dismayed he mixed now with spectres that haſtened back to the world; and thus he returned to the caſtle, where his body, neglected, lay ſtill on the dunghill, an horror to the clown and the milkmaid.

CANTO III.

LONG had dark night with mighty wings ſpread all her ſhades over the world and the village. The frightened clock ſtruck twelve, that awful hour, when ſpectres roam about with rattling chains, with fiery eyes, and in dreadful forms. Dead ſilence reigned in the Gothic caſtle; old Raban and his niece, the cook and the coachmen, and the houſemaids all lay buried deep in ſleep, except prim Betty, who lovingly awake, employed her needle at the light of the nightly lamp, embroidering ruffles for her dear black John the ranger; when lo! the midnight hour refounded through the lonely caſtle. Her needle dropt at once from her trembling hands; ſhe took her ruſhlight, haſtening frightened to the ſpiral ſtair. But fear miſled her ſteps. Inſtead of running to the upper ſtory, and to her ſnug and homely cell, ſhe

hurried

hurried downward to the musty cellars dreary vaults, which long disused, waste and horrid, were now the gloomy dwellings of inauspicious bats, of rats, of ghosts and of spectres. Here doleful shrieks and sighs were often heard in awful midnight hours; and Jack the coachman had beheld there blueish lights with glittering treasures. The frighten'd maid stopt at the entrance, thunder-struck; cold panic terror seized the nymph and raised her hair; with horror she fled back again up stairs, and was just safely landing in her chamber door, when Tabby's shadow flew against her, fierce and wild. She saw his sparkling eyes, how grim he spit and gnashed his teeth; and with a shriek she plunged into her bed. And---there she lay for three long horrid hours, overwhelmed with fear and feathers, from under which she never dared to lift her head; till with the rising dawn of day, sleep did begin to visit and to pity her.

But Tabby's shadow hastened to the bedroom of old Raban; he roared for vengeance, and leapt furious on the table, from which the night-lamp spread her faint and dying rays. The trembling flame blazed up once more and Tabby's dying shrieks and howlings sounded through the dark apartment. The old man started from his sleep and looked aghast; he saw the fiery eyes of Tabby, blowing hellish flames from his nostrils. Terrible he opened his mouth and squalled aloud. The howling yelled through the castlehalls till the ghost

E   disappeared.

disappeared. With terrors less he flew to Rosaura's chamber: He appeared there in a dream, with countenance pale. "Fair "Rosaura," he said, "grant pardon to thy Tabby, if unwilling, "he breaks in upon thy slumbers; forgive a ghost, rejected on "the banks of black Cocytus, deprived now of rest and of "home, because his body lies unburied on the dunghill; nor "have his bones found any pity or a covering of dust. Ah! "could thy favourite deserve such usage? Is it for having "kindly kissed your hands, for having constantly concealed, to "you my fangs? Am I denied the indulgence of a grave, that "I waged loyal war against the rats, the enemies you most "abhorred? Was it my fault that by the fury's arts insidious, I "was provoked against your Polly? Could I controul the in-"stinct, wherewith almighty nature prompts to murder? Was "not my painful death a full atonement for an innocent "crime? Ah, heavenly fair one; your heart is made for pity; "if Tabby pleased you, when he was alive devoted to your "service, do not permit his body to be a prey of ravenous "dogs and of ducks voracious! Grant to his bones a grave, "and to his ghost grant rest, that sulky Charon may allow "him now to pass the Stygian flood; nor he be forced longer "to skip about with other spectres, and frighten you with his "appearance." Thus Tabby's ghost, which vanished in the air.

With anxious mind Rosaura awaked, when Aurora had painted the mountains with purple. The herdsman's horn resounded in the bloomy plain. Laborious oxen dragged the plow with slow progressive steps into the fields; the early farmer hastened on his neighing poney through commons and through plow land. Thrice did Rosaura pull the bell, which shrill and sharp called Betty down. She came, still pale from all her nightly terrors; and winged were the words of the lady. " Ah, " how could we neglect to bury Tabby! I saw him in a " dream, a wretched wanderer by our neglect. I cannot plead " for my ingratitude! Why didst thou not remind me of his " bones, which lie neglected in the open air, a prey to ravenous " beasts! Fly, to the gardener, order that he take him from " the dunghill, and bury him under the lime-walk on the " river's banks." Thus Rosaura. Betty replied: " I am still " shaking from the terrors of the ghost: horrid and threat- " ening were his looks, when howling he crossed over my way! " We will bury him directly, that his apparitions may no longer " disturb us at night." She had not finished when old Raban hobbled in, and leaning on his thorny stick, burst out: " Ah! " children, let us bury him! I am dead still; for heavens! " I saw him too! like a devil, his hellish eyes were fiery, " and his nostrils snored flames——I do not want to see him " any more!

" The

The Iris of the lady hurried to the gardener, whom she thus addressed: "Come, follow me, dear Dick, and take the body "of our Tabby from the dunghill. Dig thou a grave for him "in the lime-walk on the river's banks, that he may frighten "us no longer in the castle. A florin and a glass of gin shall "well reward thee for thy trouble."

Thus Betty; and Dick followed, quickened by the spirit. He went directly to the yard, took Tabby on his shovel, and did interr him in the shade of the lime-walk. And Tabby's wandring shadow hastened down again to hell, where now he mixed in the crowds of ghosts, that thronged forward to the barge of Charon.

CANTO IV.

AND now Rosaura, arm your bosom well with courage, when with the muse you venture down to hell----to hell, which many times has frightened you when devils in red stockings and with spangled shoes danced furiously on the stage, when flames of rofin rolled over the paper walls of the abyfs, and black fmoke arofe from the caverns. If your bright eyes did not lead me through the fubterraneous night, I could not dare a fecond defcent to the gloomy plains of Erebus. To difclofe the accomplifhed fate of thy Tabby, the embolden'd mufe attends him over the Stygian floods.

Charon beheld from afar the ghoft of Tabby coming on to the banks of the river. Knowing his body was buried, he moved his barge to fhore and received him. The barge ran of itfelf to the oppofite fide where Cerberus watches the entrance of Orcus. When Tabby beheld him, with three heads furioufly gnafhing his teeth and barking at him, he flew back, bending and briftling his back, and fpitting and hiffing at him in fo antick a manner, that even ftern Charon's countenance expreffed a dawn of laughing. Cerberus, however, ftopped not his fnarling, Charon landed Tabby on the banks of Tartarus; where flily on the tips of his toes he paffed by Cerberus through the cavern, to the banks of flaming Phlegethon, which roared with fiery floods over the noify rocks. Here Tabby beheld the huge walls of brafs, and the adamantine gates, which lead to the dungeon of tortures. On an iron tower, which rifes high in the air, at the entrance, fits Tifiphone, watchful and terrible; with her whip of fnakes fhe flogs back the runaways, who defponding attempted to fly from thefe black fields of pain. Tabby

E   fhuddered

shuddered when he heard the groans and the flogging, the jarring of iron, and the rattling of heavy chains, dragged along by those wretches whom Rhadamanthus, the judge of hell, has doomed to long and cruel tortures. At once with frightful yell sprung open the adamantine gates; Alecto with burning torch sallied out, laid hold of our Tabby, and dragged him scolding to the bar of the judge, when suddenly she recollected him: "O," said she, "is it thou, the victim of my ven-
"geance? Thou shalt not see then the tortures, which rave-
"nous beasts must suffer for ages together; for know, the
"lions and bloody tigers and panthers, and all those con-
"querors and terrors of the forest are tortured here in
"different manners. Wolves are roasted at slow fires; thievish
"foxes are kept at fiery chains, see hens and chickens be-
"fore them and cannot catch them. What avails it to the
"eagle, the king of birds, that he was a monarch extolled
"and praised by poets and parasites; he is doomed here,
"for ever to sit a prisoner in a red hot cage, no better than
"a robber, though adored on earth. How could I describe
"to thee the tortures innumerable, which punish the ra-
"venous beasts, that are guilty of murther, or prey on ani-
"mals, harmless and useful! This judgment does not concern
"thee, nor those, that, armed with avenging teeth or fangs or
"bills, did employ them in the public service, to the destruc-
"tion of vermin, of rats and of mice, of snakes and of lizards,
"of

"of spiders, of snails and of caterpillars: they roam here at li-
"berty, and happy in shady groves; yet cats must not destroy
"the singing birds, the pigeons and chickens, or they are
"roasted with wolves and tortured with foxes. Happy! that fate
"did protect thee! Pursue thy journey from this river to the
"fields of blessed animals. On earth they will raise thee a noble
"monument in the lime-walks on the bank of the brook, and
"tears will be shed at thy grave." Thus Alecto. She retired; the gates shut behind her, and sulphurous smoke and blue flames arose over the pillars of brass. And Tabby marched on with bolder step through many dark passages, till he reached the fortunate groves, the blest abodes of gentler animals. Here reigns eternal spring; gentler suns shed here their mild etherial emanations; and bountiful nature has pour'd here her horn of abundance over the luxuriant fields. Through bloomy plains Lethe meanders here in soft flowing waves. Animals quaff them and drink oblivion; their natures are softened. There bathe the souls, which fate has ordained to wander into other bodies. Tabby saw amongst them the cur, now intended to inhabit the body of a needy miser. Souls of parrots played there in the floods designed for philosophers and poets, that never will dare to think for themselves; there were strutting souls of peahens for fine ladies, souls of ravens for judges, and souls of foxes for clerks and attorneys. Those of better animals enjoyed here peace, and liberty and rest and spring

eternal

eternal in their Elysian fields. The generous horse walked free and lively in the meadows; cool breezes curled his flying mane; he neighed liberty. Bloomy grounds fed the laborious bull, for ever unyoked. The harmless innocent sheep skipped playful on the sunny hills, and cropped the sweet reward of useful submission and patience. Blowing groves and forests sounded of various coloured songsters. Humming birds hung on the branches in golden clusters. The nightingale's songs re-echoed in the rosy fields, where feeling poets listened to their sighs. Canary birds filled with music the air; and the brilliant bird of the sun (the kingsfisher) warbled on the banks of the river. Tabby quaffed eagerly the Lethean flood, and his rapacious ravenous nature changed to meekness at once. Pleased he basked in the sunshine. Turtle doves and pigeons fluttered down to him familiar. He played with them, and thus he forgot his painful death, in easy expectation, that once more he might return to life, and animate a nobler body.

CANTO V.

RETURN now, Muse! from the subterraneous regions! and if thy golden lyre charms solitary hours, and if Rosaura honours thee with kind applause, hear thou with unconcern, what sentence heavy pedants, or sharp critick misses, or what dunces stiff, in consequential tye-wigs, pronounce against thee.

Dick had now covered with turf the grave of Tabby. He laid his shovel on his shoulder broad, and went with solemn silence home; thus Sextons leave the ground with slow and measured steps, well paid, when some rich miser's funeral is over, attended by some Christian jews and usurers. He passed the court yard, when Rosaura saw him; and drops of tears sprung from her heavenly eyes. Old Raban sympathized with kind compassion. At last Rosaura broke the silence sad: " Go," said she, " Betty, pay the gardener for the duty he performed " to Tabby; and let him fetch some violets, that my own hands " may strew the tomb with flowers."

So said, she took her hat, and passed the court-yard with her uncle. A row of sacred lime-trees, with some firs, are planted on the castle's ditch. Their tops are like a forest in the air; their roots are washed by the silver flood; a finer green adorns their branches.. A venerable tree, lifts taller than the rest its proud head to the skies; it branches like a forest and is the haunt of the fongfters. Thime and lavender fpread their odour and fweetened the air; the fine green carpet is enriched with thoufand ranuncules and bright flowers, embroidery which puts all art to blufh. Here lay poor Tabby; his lonely grave was fweetly fhaded as the tombs of Greece and Rome, where temples were not poifoned with the infection of the dead. Around the grave ftood fair Rofaura, and her uncle, and with them Dick the gardner, Betty and black John the ranger. Rofaura took two handsful of frefh violets, and ftrewed them on the favourite's tomb; and John the ranger took the bugle horn from his fhoulders and founded through the grove the lamentation of the fportfmen, when poor Pufs or when old Reynard falls. It rouzed the dogs. They chimed in; and the cats met on the roofs and mewed in difharmonious tones to the dirge of their faithful companion; whilft the rats and the mice in their holes, rejoiced and gambol'd on the fall of dread Tabby. At laft Rofaura turning from the grave, was heard to fay, " Reft undifturbed in the fhade of the lime! " Had the Mufes adorned my brow with their bays, or in- " ftructed fomebody of this village in the language of Gods, " thy name fhould go to ftars, be exalted to the fkies, and " be beloved and dear to pofterity." Thus Rofaura, when returning to her apartment.

But

But Fame, with her trumpet, went through the village and funk down on the cottage of the church-clerk, who, with gravity majeſtic was teaching the children of the village. They hummed and ſtammered in noiſy confuſion, their repeated hard leſſons of ſpelling. Him the Goddeſs approached and addreſſed: " Thou favourite of Apollo, art thou ſilent at the death of her " ladyſhip's Tabby? Canſt thou neglect thus this call for celebrity " immortal? Was nature ſo laviſh in vain with her gift, thy poe-" tical talent, which thou ſo often exerted in New-years-day " rhimes, or poetical inſcriptions of houſes and of barns? What " prevents thee at preſent from making ſome verſes in honour " of Tabby?"

Thus ſhe kindled the poetical fire in the breaſt of the clerk, who aroſe from his cracking throne, which was made of reed. He proclaimed a furlough or holiday to his noiſy congrega-tion. As the herd of goſſipping geeſe, purſued by a playful ſpaniel, wing their vociferous flight over the pond into the reeds; thus the boys thronged noiſy from the muſty priſon, and flew to the place, where the elaſtic ball was driven into the air, with ſhouting and jubilee. But the ſchoolmaſter laid down his faſces, his birch rod and his hazel ſtick: he fixed them againſt the ſweating windows. Left to himſelf, he took his magic pen; with wrinkled brow he rolled his eyes, and launched into deep meditations for rhimes. Three times he threw his half-eaten pen to the ground; three times he invoked the muſes and his dic-
tionary.

tionary of rhimes. At laſt he ſtarted up with delight; well pleaſed he read to the aſtoniſhed walls his epitaph of Tabby. Kind Muſe, thou knoweſt it; rehearſe it to aftertimes, if thou be not afraid of the jingle of rhimes, which are as follows:

> Here lieth in ſacred reſt
> Alas! now dead and bleſt,
> A faithful TABBY, noble by deſcent,
> A good companion and a ſteady friend,
> Full well deſerving of a Monument;
> For he ſtood high in Lady ROSEY's grace,
> Which proved his worth, his virtue, and his praiſe.
> In honour of his name I wrote this down,
> The well-known pariſh-clerk, JOHN MATTHIEW FROWN.

And he wrote it clean, painting rather than writing, on ſolemn paper, ornamented with black edges, with ſkulls and with bones. He gave a bruſh to his wig, and haſtened in the pride of an author to the manor, where with countenance grave and an aukward bow he humbly delivered his ſcroll into the lady's own hands. Smiling ſhe peruſed his rhimes, and added: " In honour of Tabby " I will have it in marble, a monument of his fate. Two " ſilver dollars muſt reward the worthy poet." She ſaid it, and ſent the ranger to the maſon, who cut it in marble. It covers the tomb, which is ſhut now for ever. The viſitor ſees it well pleaſed, and curious wanderers tell of the eloquent ſtone in their countries. Thus Tabby's name was exalted to the ſtars; and lateſt poſterity will reſound his Fame.

F I N I S.

Printed by Libri Plureos GmbH in Hamburg, Germany